MARY ENGELBREIT

CRAFTS TO DECORATE YOUR HOME

Meredith® Press
Des Moines, Iowa

Meredith® Press
An imprint of Meredith® Books

Mary Engelbreit: Crafts to Decorate Your Home
Editor: Carol Field Dahlstrom
Technical Editor: Susan M. Banker
Graphic Designer: Angie Hoogensen
Copy Chief: Catherine Hamrick
Copy and Production Editor: Terri Fredrickson
Contributing Proofreaders: Colleen Johnson,
 Margaret Smith
Photographers: Andy Lyons Cameraworks, Scott Little
Technical Illustrator: Chris Neubauer Graphics, Inc.
Electronic Production Coordinator: Paula Forest
Editorial and Design Assistants: Judy Bailey,
 Mary Lee Gavin, Karen Schirm
Production Director: Douglas M. Johnston
Production Manager: Pam Kvitne
Assistant Prepress Manager: Marjorie J. Schenkelberg

Meredith® Books
Editor in Chief: James D. Blume
Design Director: Matt Strelecki
Managing Editor: Gregory H. Kayko

Director, Sales & Marketing, Retail:
 Michael A. Peterson
Director, Sales & Marketing, Special Markets:
 Rita McMullen
Director, Sales & Marketing, Home & Garden Center
 Channel: Ray Wolf
Director, Operations: George A. Susral

Vice President, General Manager: Jamie L. Martin

Meredith Publishing Group
President, Publishing Group: Christopher M. Little
Vice President, Consumer Marketing & Development:
 Hal Oringer

Meredith Corporation
Chairman and Chief Executive Officer: William T. Kerr

Chairman of the Executive Committee: E. T. Meredith III

Cover Illustration: Mary Engelbreit Studios

All of us at Meredith® Press are dedicated to providing you with information and ideas to create beautiful and useful projects. We welcome your comments and suggestions. Write to us at: Meredith® Press, Crafts Editorial Department, 1716 Locust St., Des Moines, IA 50309-3023.

If you would like to purchase copies of any of our books, check wherever quality books are sold.

about mary

One of America's most popular illustrators, Mary Engelbreit has attracted millions of passionate fans with her richly illustrated designs for greeting cards, posters, gifts, and home accents. Her warmhearted style is reminiscent of old-fashioned storybooks— the colors are luminous, the designs ornate. Each illustration is a window to a dazzling world where you can get happily lost. Mary shows us a world where goodness prevails and has transferred her trademarked chubby-cheeked children, black-and-white checkered borders, cherries, and cozy corners to products that capture the eyes and hearts of people everywhere.

In addition to being America's most beloved greeting card artist, Mary is the author of a weekly newspaper column and editor in chief of a bi-monthly magazine, Mary Engelbreit's Home Companion. She lives in St. Louis, Missouri, with her husband and two children.

Mary shares her extraordinary talent by providing the inspiration for all the crafts you see in this book—crafts you can make to decorate your home.

contents

CHAPTER 1 COME TO THE TABLE

Set the table in style or pull up to the counter on a stool that's cheery any time of the day—that's just what you'll do with this chapter filled with the whimsy of Mary Engelbreit.

CHAPTER 2 LET THE LIGHT SHINE

Bright ideas await with loads of creative lighting projects to make—from candles that shine like stars in the night to lamps that are charming all day long.

CHAPTER 3 CUDDLE UP COMFORT

Create clever afghans, pillows, and stools that are guaranteed to "cozy up" your home, lending warmth and comfort for all to enjoy.

CHAPTER 4 COME OUTSIDE WITH ME

The garden, the backyard, the front porch—you're invited to craft a "how'd you ever do that!" sensation that your neighbors will love as much as you do.

CHAPTER 5 TREAT YOUR WINDOWS

From imaginative valances and tiebacks to curtains beaming with personality plus, these sun-kissed window treatments will create the finishing touch to any room.

CHAPTER 6 LITTLE EXTRAS

Whether you want to paint a glass cherry jar or transform a frame into a work of art, you'll learn new techniques to add special touches throughout your home sweet home.

a few of my favorite things

Our homes are indeed our castles and we should surround ourselves with our favorite things. Sometimes these are things we have purchased, but oftentimes they are special items we make ourselves—crafts that show our personal style.

We create our environments by making things that please us—in colors that make us feel the way we want to feel. That's why we've provided you with three color palettes in this book—to fit your own personal needs and to show off your decorating personality. I love certain combinations of colors like red, white, and black; tan and green; yellow and red. (Right now my house is done in tan and green—but that could change at any moment!)

Every room should reflect your tastes—and by crafting your own accessories you can make each corner of your home a special one. I'm sure you have a favorite room in your home just as I do. My spot is my studio where I can sit and dream. I surround myself with my favorite things to inspire me.

My sun-filled studio is my favorite spot.

In this book of project ideas and inspirations, we've included clever ideas for tabletops, window treatments, crafts to decorate outside (such as garden, deck, and patio accessories) and little extras for every room of the house. I love to showcase my collections all through the house. (I have a weakness for products from the 1920s and 1930s—especially children's books and toys.) Some of the crafts (such as the cherry jars on pages 98–99 or the teacup candles on pages 40–41) could be added to your favorite collections already on display.

It seems I'm always relying on frames and pillows to accessorize many of the rooms in my home. The frames are so important to display my cherished photos and I love pillows everywhere—they make a home even more cozy and warm. I especially like the frames with decoupaged mats on pages 102–103.

We've included all kinds of crafts to decorate your home that we hope will make your home a bit more personal, more playful, more lovely—more you. And if you learn a new crafting technique along the way on this decorating adventure, we're glad of that, too.

Everyone needs their own spot and we hope yours is filled with favorite things—wonderful crafts you've made yourself to decorate your home.

Mary Engelbreit

come
to the
table

When you call your busy family to the table, they'll come in a hurry
to see what you've created! From delightfully checkered place mats
and brightly painted snack trays to sit-up-straight bar stools and
terrific tabletop topiaries, in this chapter you'll find ideas to make
your home a clever and cozy haven.

Checkerboard Place Mat

Button flowers bloom on these checkerboard mats made of woven ribbons and edged in bits of felt. Adjust the dimensions easily for an eye-catching mat of any size.

WHAT YOU'LL NEED
Scissors
3 yards of 1½-inch-wide grosgrain
    ribbon in desired color
3 yards of 1½-inch-wide grosgrain
    ribbon in contrasting color
15x15-inch piece of corrugated
    cardboard or ¼-inch-thick
    foam board
Push pins
Straight pins
6x6-inch piece of felt in desired color
6x6-inch piece of felt in a second color
Transparent sewing machine thread
Tracing paper
Scraps of green felt
White or ivory cotton embroidery floss
12½x12½-inch piece of felt for backing
Round buttons in an assortment of
    colors and sizes

OPPOSITE Black and white ribbons
create a graphic background for
colorful button flowers.

ABOVE The pastel version of this
mat has lavender edging all around
instead of alternating felt colors.

ABOVE RIGHT An unexpected
purple and burgundy felt edging adds
pizzazz to the neutral colored mat.

OUR THREE VERSIONS
For bright color scheme
Black, white, fuchsia, lime green,
yellow, red, orange, and purple
For pastel color scheme
Lavender, light blue, lime green,
white, dark pink, and light pink
For neutral color scheme
Tan, ivory, burgundy, purple, dark
green, and brown

Checkerboard Place Mat

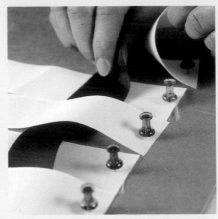

HERE'S HOW

▲ **1.** Cut seven 14-inch-long pieces from both colors of ribbon. Using one color of ribbon, lay the ribbons side by side with the ends aligned. Secure one end of the ribbons to cardboard or foam board using push pins.

▲ **2.** Weave the other color of ribbon over and under the secured ribbons. After the weaving is completed, pin all of the edges in place and remove the mat from the piece of cardboard. Fold all ribbon ends to the back and pin.

▲ **3.** Cut twenty eight 1½-inch squares from the felt pieces, 16 from the first color and the remaining 12 from the contrasting color. Turning the felt edging pieces on point as shown above, pin them to the mat edge, alternating colors, if desired. Machine-stitch the felt squares to the mat edge, stitching ¼ inch from the edge.

4. Trace the leaf patterns, *opposite*, onto tracing paper. Cut them out. Use the patterns to cut five large leaves and two small leaves from green felt. Referring to the photos, *pages 10–11*, as a guide, stitch the leaves to the mat corner with embroidery floss and long straight stitches (see diagram, *opposite*).

5. Stack two buttons as desired and sew on top of the leaves. Knot the floss on top of buttons and trim the ends.

▲ **6.** Pin the large piece of felt to the back of the woven mat. Sew on the backing piece with whipstitches (see diagram, *opposite*).

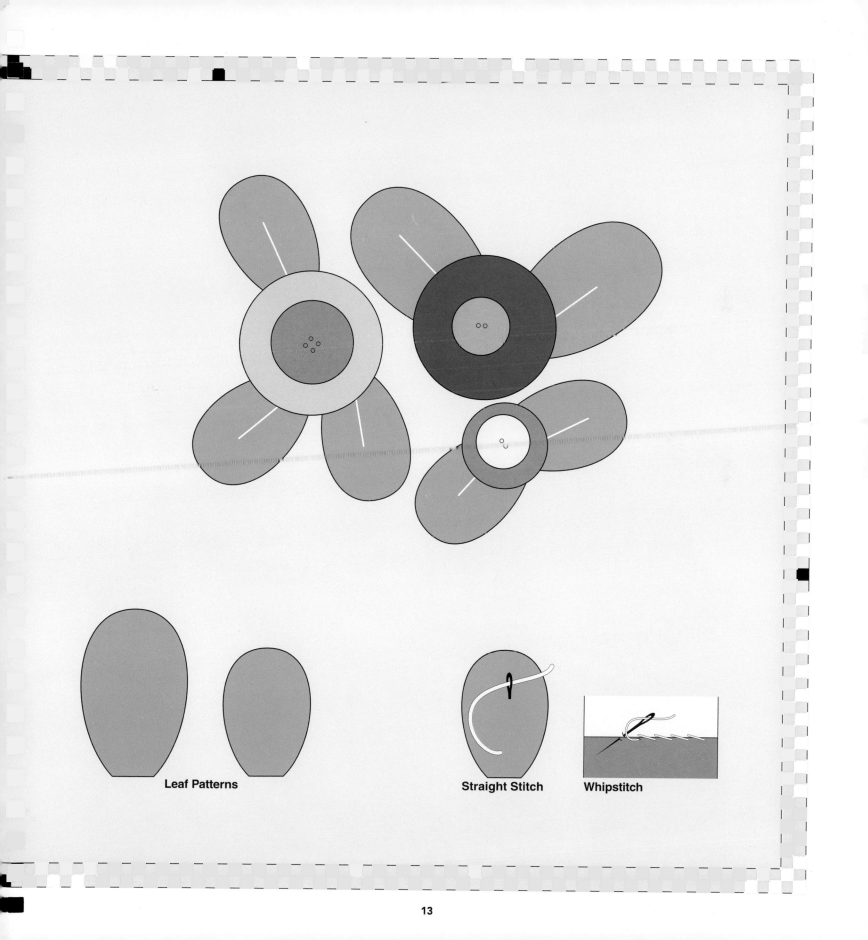

Leaf Patterns

Straight Stitch

Whipstitch

Perfectly Painted Snack Trays

Vintage clear glassware makes a grand comeback when accented with dabs of colorful glass paints on the "already there" pattern.

WHAT YOU'LL NEED

Clear glassware such as snack
trays, plates, and coffee cups
Smooth-surfaced flatware
Dish soap and water
Rubbing alcohol
Liquitex® Glossies High Gloss
Acrylic Enamel
Foam plates to use for palettes
Pencil with round-tip eraser
Small round paintbrush
Oven, if desired

OPPOSITE This snack set had a
leaf design in the glass that made
it easy to highlight the shapes
using green paint.

ABOVE RIGHT Perfect polka dots
were achieved by dipping a round
pencil-tip eraser in copper paint and
dabbing it gently on the surfaces of
the dishes and flatware.

BOTTOM RIGHT The circle designs in
these dishes look like colorful candies
when painted in bright glass paints.

HERE'S HOW

1. Wash the glassware and flatware in
dish soap and warm water. For best
paint adhesion, clean the surfaces again
with rubbing alcohol. After washing, do
not touch the areas to be painted.

2. To create polka dots, squeeze a
small amount of paint onto a plate.
Dip a round pencil-tip eraser into the
paint. Gently dab the paint, where
desired, on the back of the glassware
or on the flatware handles. *(Note: Be
sure to paint only on areas where food
or liquid will not come in contact.)*
Create as many polka dots as desired.
Let the paint dry.

3. To add paint to indentations in
glass, use a small round paintbrush to
paint the areas on the back of the
glassware. Let the paint dry.

4. To make the painted glassware
and flatware durable and dishwasher
safe, place the pieces in the oven and
bake at 325° for 40 minutes in a
well-ventilated room. *Do not* remove
the glassware or flatware pieces until
they have cooled completely in the oven.

OUR THREE VERSIONS

For the neutral color scheme
Copper
For the bright color scheme
Bright pink, yellow, and green
For the natural color scheme
Green

Embellished Bar Stools

You'll be sittin' pretty when you cozy up to the breakfast bar on one of these whimsically painted stools.

WHAT YOU'LL NEED
Newspapers
Purchased wooden stool
White spray primer
Paintbrushes
Acrylic paints in desired colors
Paper towels
Soft pencil in any color
Ruler
Clear acrylic varnish

OUR THREE VERSIONS
For primary color scheme
Yellow ochre, red, bright lime
green, blue, hot pink, lavender,
medium purple, black, and white
For pastel color scheme
Pink, soft yellow, light lime green,
medium pale green, lavender, baby
blue, white, and black
For bright color scheme
Orange, plum, olive green, yellow
ochre, rust brown, black, and white

OPPOSITE AND ABOVE Vibrant
primary colors and charming
floral motifs pop off the dancing
polka-dot background.

TOP RIGHT Single blooms painted in
pastel colors add a feminine touch to
this stool.

BOTTOM RIGHT Small and large
flowers pair up as pretty accents in the
black squares.

Embellished Bar Stools

HERE'S HOW

1. In a well-ventilated area, cover the work surface with newspapers. Place the stool in the center of the newspapers and spray the entire stool with a white spray primer. Spray two light coats. Allow the primer to dry.

2. Paint the inside of the legs first, using the desired color. Use a good quality wide flat brush for acrylic paint. The paint can overlap onto the horizontal spindles and outer edges of legs as it can be painted over easily. Rinse the paintbrush well when changing colors, and wipe off excess water onto a paper towel.

3. Paint the outside of the legs the desired color, carefully and neatly where the two colors meet. Paint the horizontal spindles.

4. Paint the top surface of the stool seat a flat background color or sponge paint the surface, if desired. The paint can overlap onto the sides a little.

5. Paint the rim of stool seat the lighter color first, neatly trimming the edge where the colors meet.

6. Now that all surfaces have the base colors painted, decorate the stool legs with dots, stripes, flowers, lines, hearts, or other designs.

▲**7.** To draw the squares on the seat, find the center point of the circle. Using a ruler and very soft pencil, draw a light line dividing the circle in half.

Draw another light line extending from the center at a 90° angle. Measure and draw a 2½x2½-inch square in the center. Draw parallel lines every 2½ inches. Use a square-cornered piece of paper as a guide to draw the lines.

▲**8.** Paint alternate squares with the contrasting color of paint.

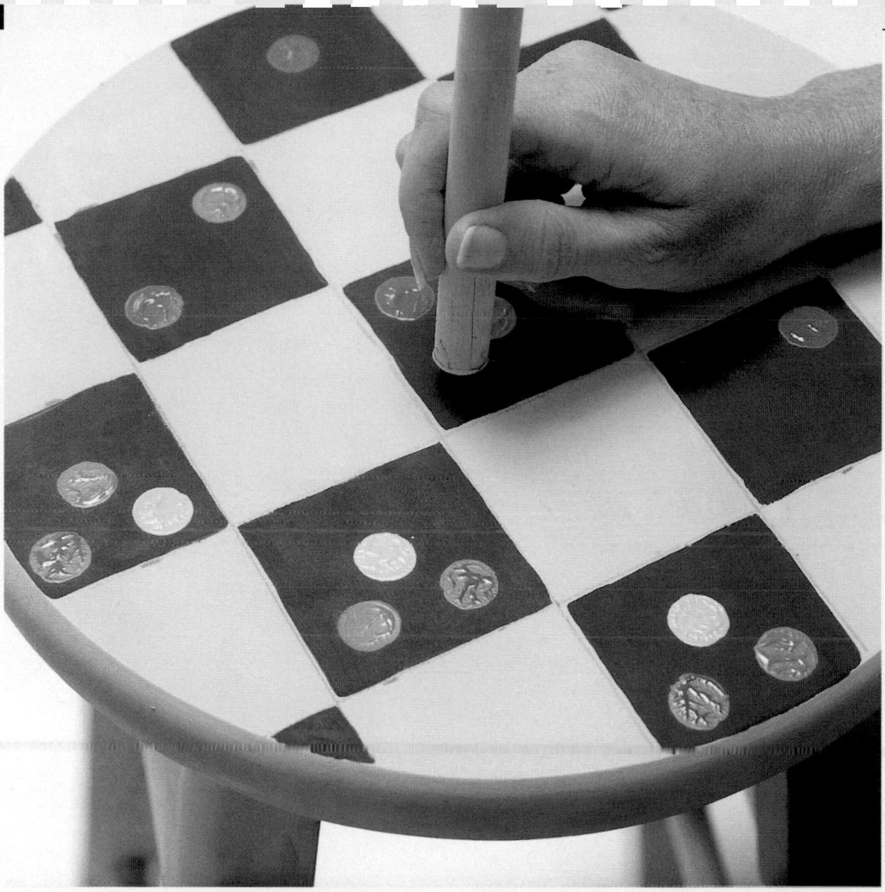

▲ **9.** Paint four or five flowers in the desired squares (or adapt the design as shown on *page 17*) by dipping a dowel in paint and dotting it on the surface.

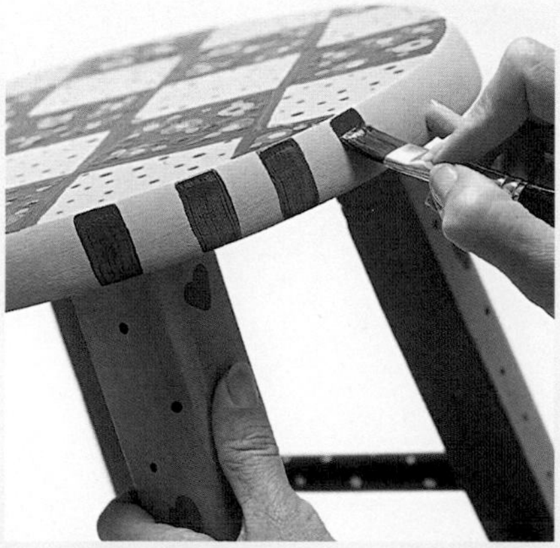

10. Add centers to the flowers and leaves as desired.

11. Outline the squares with a contrasting color. The lines do not have to be perfectly even or straight.

◀ **12.** To add stripes to the rim of the seat, use a flat brush to paint vertical lines along the rim using the darker paint color.

13. Apply a clear non-yellowing spray varnish to the entire stool. Let the varnish dry completely.

Buying and painting furniture

✻ Look for stools and other unfinished furniture in home improvement centers and discount and crafts stores.

✻ If using a flea-market find, be sure to strip any existing finish from the piece of furniture and prime the wood before painting.

✻ For a weathered look, sand the edges of the furniture piece after the paint is thoroughly dry.

✻ If the stool or other furniture piece is unpainted but has a varnish finish, use a fine sandpaper or steel wool to buff the surfaces before painting.

Fancy Fruit Topiaries

Cluster miniature fruits together to make towering topiaries that bring summertime bounty indoors to enjoy year-round.

WHAT YOU'LL NEED
Acrylic paints
Paintbrush
⅝-inch-diameter dowel, cut to
   12 inches long
5-inch terra-cotta flower pot saucer
5-inch Styrofoam™ ball
Styrofoam to fit in saucer
Thick white crafts glue
3 yards of narrow ribbons
Miniature artificial fruits
T-pins or stick pins
Colored raffia

OPPOSITE Bright red cherries nestle
in a black-and-white polka-dot base.

BELOW Orange ribbons add
even more color to this tiny
tree bearing lemons and limes.

OUR THREE VERSIONS
For the cherries scheme
Black, white, yellow, red, and green
For the citrus scheme
Yellow, orange, and green
For the grapes scheme
Lavender, mauve, and soft
moss green

BELOW RIGHT Grape clusters look
real with artificial leaves peeking
through here and there.

Fancy Fruit Topiaries

HERE'S HOW

1. Paint the dowel and clay saucer (see photos, *opposite*). With the end of a paintbrush dipped in paint, add dots on the saucer. If the Styrofoam is white, paint it green. Let all pieces dry.

▲ **3.** Wind ribbons around the dowel to create stripes. Secure the ribbons with glue.

▶ **4.** Glue the fruits onto the Styrofoam ball. Begin at the top and work downward. Secure with pins until the glue is dry.

▲ **2.** Insert the dowel into the center of the Styrofoam ball to about 3½ inches deep. Glue a piece of Styrofoam into the clay saucer. Allow it to set and insert the dowel into the center of the saucer reinforcing it with glue. Let the glue dry.

5. Coat the Styrofoam base in the saucer with a generous amount of glue. Wind the raffia around and around the dowel until the entire surface is covered well. Use T-pins to hold the raffia in place until the glue dries.

6. Finish the topiary with a generous ribbon bow tied below the top. Using different colors of ribbon, loop strands back and forth, leaving tails on both sides. Tie the ribbons tightly in the center with a 10-inch piece of ribbon and tie around the dowel at the top. Trim the tails if needed.

Folk Art Mats

Embellish this oh-so-fun machine-appliquéd design with embroidery stitches to make cheerful place mats for your breakfast nook.

WHAT YOU'LL NEED

Fusible interfacing; pencil

8x8-inch piece of blue calico fabric for bird; 6x6 inch piece of contrasting blue calico fabric for bird's wing

6x6-inch piece each of four different calico fabrics for flowers

4x4-inch piece of green calico fabric for leaves

Two 13x18-inch pieces of fabric for background and backing

Rayon twist thread for machine embroidery in colors to match fabrics

¼ yard of contrasting fabric for binding

13x18-inch piece of fleece

Cotton embroidery floss in green, orange, black, and two coordinating colors for flower details

HERE'S HOW

1. Trace each pattern piece from *page 27* onto fusible interfacing according to the manufacturer's directions. Fuse the shapes to the coordinating fabrics as listed *above*.

2. Cut out and fuse the shapes atop each other and to the background fabric using the placement pattern, *page 26*, as a guide.

3. Machine satin-stitch (a close zigzag) the pieces to the background fabric using rayon twist threads that match the fabric colors.

4. Referring to the diagrams on *page 26*, work the specialty stitches. Use two plies of green floss and stem stitches to create the flower stems. Work the bird's feet in satin stitches using two plies of orange, outlining the feet using a stem stitch. Work the flower details with straight stitches and French knots using three plies. Work a satin stitch eye using two plies of black.

5. Place the fleece atop the backing fabric. Place the appliquéd piece, right side up, over the fleece. Stitch the layers together ¼ inch from the edges.

6. From binding fabric, cut two 2½x19-inch binding strips and two 2½x14-inch strips. Fold under ¼ inch on each long edge and press. Fold the binding in half lengthwise and press.

7. Pin binding to mat front, right sides together, so the edge of the binding is 1 inch from the edge of the mat. Stitch the front of binding to the mat. Miter and stitch the corners. Use whipstitches to tack the back binding to the mat.

OPPOSITE Sky blue trim sets off this mat embellished with hand stitches.

ABOVE RIGHT These yellow and orange colors are as warm as summer's sunshine.

BELOW RIGHT Soft calicos and plaids give this mat a country look.

OUR THREE VERSIONS

For bright blue color scheme
Bright blue, lime green, yellow, bright pink, orange, white, and turquoise
For sunny color scheme
Yellow, orange, green, and blue
For mauve color scheme
Mauve, blue, green, and gold

French Knot

Satin Stitch

Stem Stitch

Straight Stitch

Bird and Flower Patterns

let
the
light
shine

Enhance the ambience in any room with wonderful lamps and clever

candles. Whether you need an inviting centerpiece for your next

gathering, or a colorful luminaria to guide your way, these lighting

ideas will leave you glowing with fresh and fun ideas.

Beaded Lampshades

Here's a new twist for turning a plain-Jane lampshade into one that really shines.

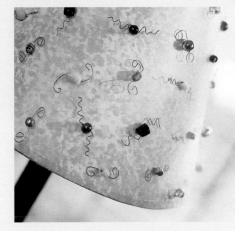

WHAT YOU'LL NEED
Pencil; ruler; acrylic paints; paper plate
Paintbrush; natural sea sponge and
   water (optional)
Purchased lampshade
Large safety pin; assorted beads
Silver or gold beading wire
Needle-nose pliers

OUR THREE VERSIONS
For striped scheme
Lavender, purple, teal, and white paint
Purple and teal beads with gold wire
For yellow color scheme
Yellow and white paint
Neutral color beads with silver wire
For mauve color scheme
Mauve and white paint
Gold, mauve, and white beads and
brass wire

HERE'S HOW
1. Use a pencil and ruler to mark desired vertical stripes on the shade. Paint the stripes the desired color. Paint the remaining triangular shapes a contrasting color. Use a flat brush to paint a ½-inch-wide white stripe around the bottom edge. When dry, use the same size brush to paint the darker colored checks every ½ inch. If a sponged background is desired, put a small amount of each paint on a paper plate. Dip a dampened sponge into each paint color and dab on plate. Dab paint on the lampshade until the shade is covered. Allow the paint to dry.
▼2. Using a safety pin, poke two holes into the shade approximately ¼ inch apart wherever beads will be placed.

▲3. Cut several 3-inch-long pieces of wire. From the inside of the shade, poke one end of wire through a hole made from the safety pin. Put on a bead and lace the wire through the second hole. Twist the wire ends together on the inside of the shade. *To have the wire ends show,* lace the wire piece through the shade with the ends on the outside. Place one, two, or three beads on one end of the wire. Bring the opposite wire end back through the beads in the opposite direction. Pull both wire ends tight.

OPPOSITE Stripes and checks provide a festive background for iridescent beads secured in place with wire.

ABOVE LEFT Sponge-painted in yellow and white, this shade is accented with natural-tone beads and gold wire, twisted into coils and zigzags.

ABOVE RIGHT This lamp is topped with a sponged shade that has golden and swirled beads grouped together.

Use a needle-nose pliers to twist the wire ends into spiral and zigzag shapes. Attach beads until the desired look is achieved.

Summer-Porch Luminarias

For a touch of nostalgia on warm evenings, set these welcoming

luminarias on the porch or deck, or in the garden.

WHAT YOU'LL NEED

Tracing paper
Pencil
Masking tape
Decorative watering can in desired size
Large nail
Water
Towel
Hammer
Waxed paper
Spray paint
Candle to fit watering can

OUR THREE VERSIONS

For checkerboard luminaria
Soft lavender
For star luminaria
Yellow-ochre
For dragonfly luminaria
Country turquoise

OPPOSITE Transform watering cans into glowing luminarias by punching designs into the sides. Use citronella candles to keep the bugs away from your garden party.

HERE'S HOW

1. Trace desired pattern from pages 34–35 onto tracing paper. Cut out pattern, leaving about ½ inch of blank paper on the top and bottom.

▲**2.** Use masking tape to attach the pattern to the watering can where the pattern is desired.

3. Use a nail to mark the design onto the watering can by pressing the nail on each dot. Remove the pattern.

4. Fill the watering can with water and place it in the freezer. If the decorative can leaks, place a plastic sandwich bag inside of the can before filling. The water should freeze completely.

▲**5.** Lay the watering can on a towel so it won't roll. To punch the holes for the design, place the nail over one of the indentations previously marked. Gently tap the hammer until the nail penetrates the watering can, marking the design. Repeat until the entire design has been punched. Rinse ice away with warm water. Dry the watering can.

6. Cover the work surface in a well-ventilated area with waxed paper and place the watering can in the center of the paper. Spray paint the watering can the desired color. Let the paint dry. Place a candle inside the watering can.

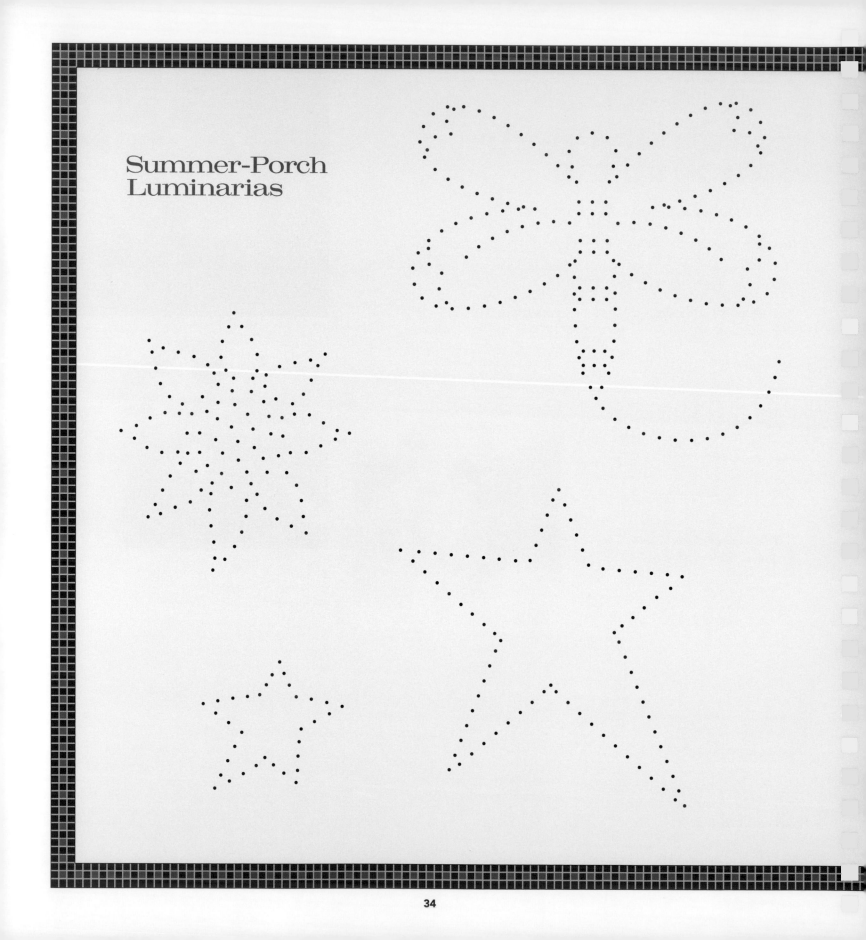

Summer-Porch Luminarias

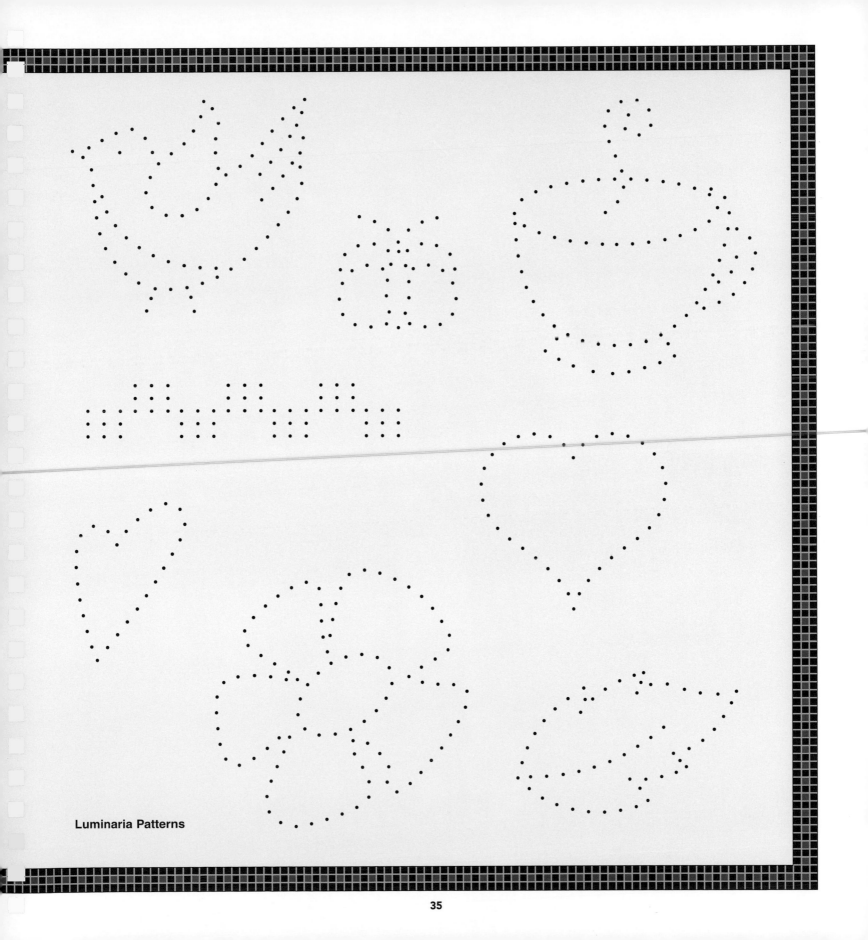

Luminaria Patterns

Shimmering Screen Lampshades

Hardly hardware any more—ordinary window screen finds a new home atop a taper and holder.

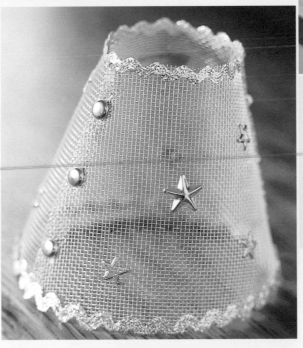

WHAT YOU'LL NEED

Tracing paper
One foot of wire window
  screen
Black marker
Old scissors
Metallic gold spray paint
Trims, such as star studs
  and buttons
Thin wire, if desired
Paper clips
Brass candle follower
Awl
Six ½-inch-long brass paper
  fasteners
Rickrack or braid
Thick white crafts glue

OUR THREE VERSIONS

For vintage scheme
Red buttons
Red rickrack
For star-studded scheme
Silver rickrack
Gold star studs
For polka-dot button scheme
Yellow and white buttons
Navy braid

OPPOSITE Spray painted metallic gold, this shade gets even fancier trimmed with vintage buttons and wide rickrack.

ABOVE Star studs and rickrack adorn this silver screen shade.

ABOVE RIGHT Buttons are wired to this shade to suggest a casual polka-dot motif.

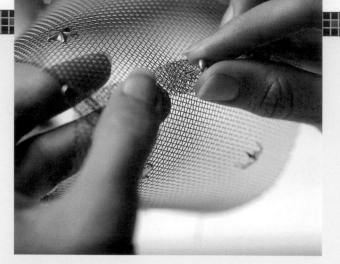

Shimmering Screen Lampshades

HERE'S HOW

1. Trace the full-size pattern, *opposite*, and cut it out. Lay the pattern on top of the wire screen and trace around it twice with a black marker. Cut out the two pieces and spray both sides of each piece with spray paint, allowing to dry between coats.

2. Fold over the left side of each piece ⅜ inch, creasing the edge.

▲ **3.** If using star studs, attach them randomly on each section by bringing the prongs to the back side and folding them to the center to secure on the screen. If adding buttons, attach with a thin piece of wire threaded through the holes, twisting the ends together on the back to secure.

4. Join the two sections together by overlapping the sides, making sure the folded edge of each section is on top. Use paper clips to hold the tops and bottoms of the sections together. Slip the shade over the candle follower to check for a good fit. Make adjustments by changing the overlapped edges. Remove the shade from the follower.

▼ **5.** Using an awl, poke a hole ½ inch up from the bottom edge and again ½ inch down from the top edge on one of the overlapped sides.

▲ **6.** Insert a paper fastener into each hole and fold the ends of the fastener down against the inside of the shade. Poke a third hole in the center of the overlapped edge and insert a third fastener. Repeat for the other overlapped side.

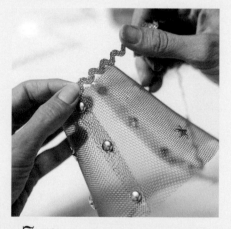

▲ **7.** Glue trim around top and bottom edge of the shade. Allow the glue to dry. Trim any stray pieces of wire that might extend beyond the edges.

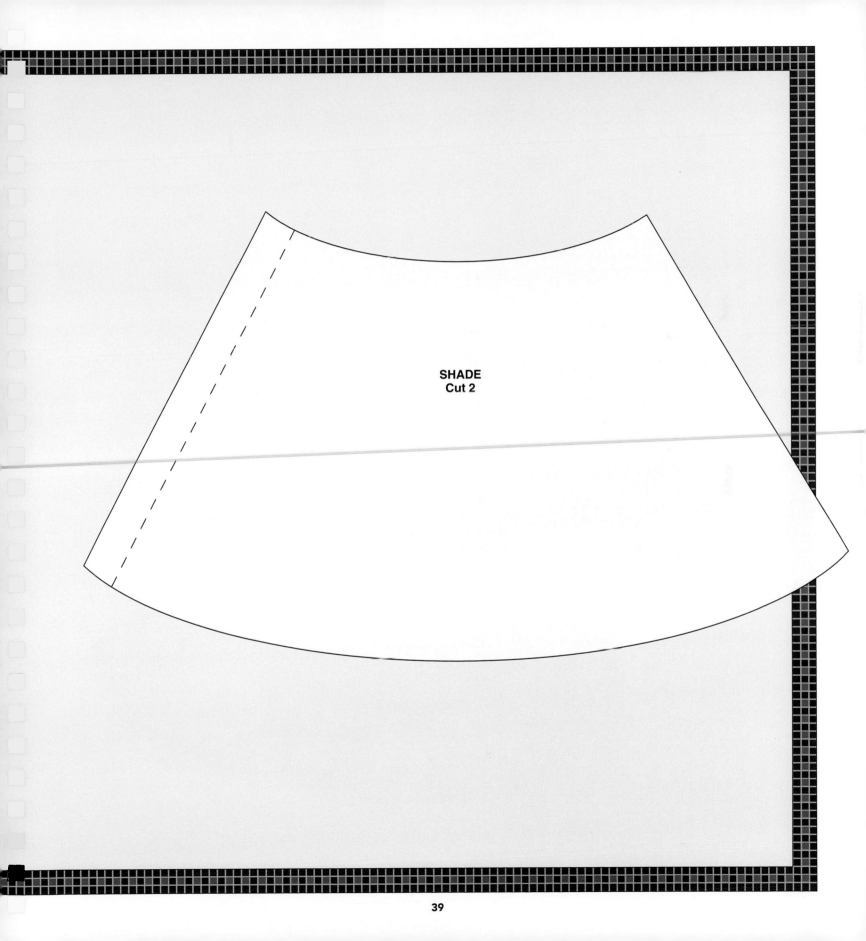

SHADE
Cut 2

Teacup Candles

Tea with a friend can become an unforgettable celebration when the table is aglow with these teacup treasures.

WHAT YOU'LL NEED
Teacup
Candle wax
White birthday candles
Trims, such as beads, ribbon, pearls on a string, and buttons
Thick white crafts glue

HERE'S HOW
1. Pour hot water into the teacups to warm them.
2. To melt the wax, set a coffee can in a pan of water on the stove or hot plate. Break up the wax and place it in the coffee can. Let the wax melt and remove it from the heat.
3. Pour the water out of the teacups and dry thoroughly. Carefully pour the hot wax into the cups and let them set until a soft covering appears on the top of the wax (about two or three minutes). Push a birthday candle into the wax and steady it until it stands up straight.
4. Glue trims to the cup and saucer as desired.

OUR THREE VERSIONS
For yellow scheme
Yellow, blue, red, white, black, green, and pink
For pastel color scheme
White, dark peach, gold, and light aqua
For red scheme
Red, yellow, black, and white

OPPOSITE Tiny glass beads parade around the cup and saucer rims while a striking floral border is achieved by grouping together a handful of colorful beads and buttons.

ABOVE LEFT Edged in pearls, this dainty cup is accented with heart buttons and round gold beads.

ABOVE RIGHT A small bow glued to the teacup handle adds the perfect finishing touch.

cuddle up
comfort

Home is where we go to relax, rejuvenate, and dream. This chapter helps you do that by showing you how to make everything from stools to rest your feet to pillowcases that will pamper you in style. These comforts of home can be yours to make and enjoy for many kick-back-and-relax days using some simple, fun techniques.

Fabulous Footstools

Put your feet up on this fancy footstool and pamper yourself in grand style.

WHAT YOU'LL NEED

Purchased wooden footstool
Fabric for cushion
Scissors
Thread
Needle
Polyfill stuffing
Acrylic paints in desired colors
Paintbrushes
Clear non-yellowing varnish
Upholstery braided or fringed trim
Thick white crafts glue
Ribbon
Button

OUR THREE VERSIONS

For the bright color scheme
Bright sunflower yellow, orange, red, lime green, and blue
For the pastel color scheme
Pale yellow, pale spring green, baby blue, and white
For the natural tone color scheme
Dark burgundy red, ochre, olive green, and black

OPPOSITE Bright primary fabrics and paints to match are oh-so-fun when accented with solid blue and orange.

ABOVE The pastel version of this stool has a white tassel skirt that softly trims the edges.

ABOVE RIGHT Rich, dark tones come to life with touches of ochre paint.

Fabulous Footstools

1. To determine how much fabric to buy, measure the top of the footstool, and add 2¼ inches to each dimension for each of two pieces. If the stool top has rounded corners, use the stool as a guide to draw the corners. To sew, place the right sides of fabric together and sew around edges, using a ½-inch seam allowance. Leave an opening for stuffing the cushion. Clip the corners or curves. Turn inside out and stuff the pillow until it is about 2 inches thick. Hand-sew the opening shut.

◄▲ **2.** If the stool needs assembly, it is much easier to paint the pieces before putting the footstool together. Use the shapes or lines in spindles or legs to create divisions of different colors. Paint the sections the background color of choice, then add designs like dots, stripes, and squares. Allow the paint to dry and finish with a coat of clear non-yellowing varnish. Allow to dry thoroughly.

◄ **3.** Cut the fringed trim to fit around the edge of the stool seat. Put a line of crafts glue on the trim and press it onto the stool edge, straightening and smoothing the trim as it is attached.

▼**4.** Cut two lengths of ribbon long enough to fit around the cushion and be tied underneath the stool seat.

▼ **5.** Cross the two ribbons in the center and attach a button with needle and thread. Find the center point of the cushion and sew the button and ribbons to the cushion. Pull the thread to the other side of the cushion and sew back through the button several times to create a little tuck. (It does not have to be tight.)

6. Place the cushion with ribbons onto the stool, bring ribbons underneath and tie firmly. Trim off the excess ribbon.

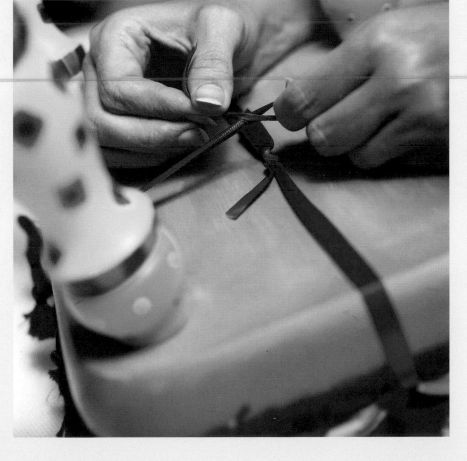

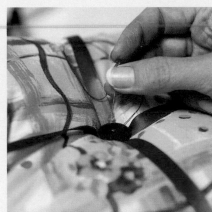

All-Star Pillow Shams

Sweet dreams and starry nights await with these fabulous felt pillow shams that add color and texture to your bed.

WHAT YOU'LL NEED

One 36x30 inch and
  one 34x28-inch piece
  of felt in desired color
One 35x29-inch piece
  of felt in coordinating
  color
Several felt squares in
  desired colors
Pencil
Tracing paper
Scissors
Straight pins
Fabric marking pencil
Sewing machine and
  thread
Fusible webbing
Iron
Damp cloth, optional
Sewing needle
Embroidery floss
Standard-size pillow
27 inches of
  self-adhesive Velcro™

OPPOSITE Bright pink felt provides a vivid background for the bold stars and tiny checks.

ABOVE For added interest, large checkered motifs accent the corners of this fun pillow sham.

ABOVE RIGHT Olive green and rust embroidery flosses outline these dancing stars in neutral colors.

OUR THREE VERSIONS

For the bright color scheme
Hot pink, bright yellow, purple, black, white, and turquoise felts, plus black and white embroidery flosses
For the jewel-tone color scheme
Deep purple, yellow, black, white, blue, and red felts, plus gold embroidery floss
For the natural color scheme
Cream, tan, olive green, orange, and rust, plus olive green and rust embroidery flosses

All-Star Pillow Shams

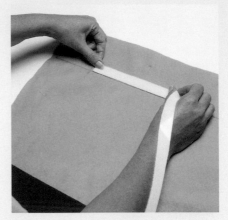

HERE'S HOW

1. On the smallest felt piece (28x34 inches) draw a temporary line 3 inches from the edge on all sides. The area inside this rectangle area is where the star-shape holes will be cut out.

▲**2.** Trace the patterns, *page 51*, onto tracing paper and cut out. Pin eight or nine of the two larger star shapes randomly onto the felt shape. When the desired look is achieved, trace around the star patterns using a fabric marking pencil. Poke scissors into the felt in center of the traced star and cut out each star shape, leaving cutout shapes in the rectangle.

3. Center the top 28x34-inch rectangle (with the star cutouts) over the 29x35-inch contrasting felt rectangle. There should be a ½-inch border of contrasting color all the way around. Pin the two pieces of felt together and sew along *one* long edge, along the drawn line.

4. Iron the fusible webbing onto the desired felt colors. Trace around the two smallest star patterns and the square patterns as many times as desired. Remove the protective paper and cut out the shapes.

▼**5.** Place the prepared felt shapes atop each other, using the photograph on *page 48* as a guide for placement. Layer various sized stars and layer squares in a check pattern. Make sure the adhesive side is placed down with the felt side up. Arrange layered shapes on sham and iron with steam or place a thin damp towel over the layered shapes and press with iron set on "wool." Continue to press with an iron until the shapes are firmly attached.

6. After ironing is finished, hand topstitch about ¼ inch from the edge around the star shapes using three strands of embroidery floss.

▲**7.** Create a closure at the top of the pillow sham. Cut a piece of adhesive-backed Velcro about 27 inches long. Adhere one side of it to the back of the middle felt piece, lining up the bottom edge of the Velcro with the seam line.

8. Pin the final 30x36-inch rectangular piece to the other finished pieces. Center all pieces on top of each other. Sew the remaining three seams on the drawn lines.

9. Position the remaining piece of Velcro on the inside back piece to match to its other half. Press firmly to adhere.

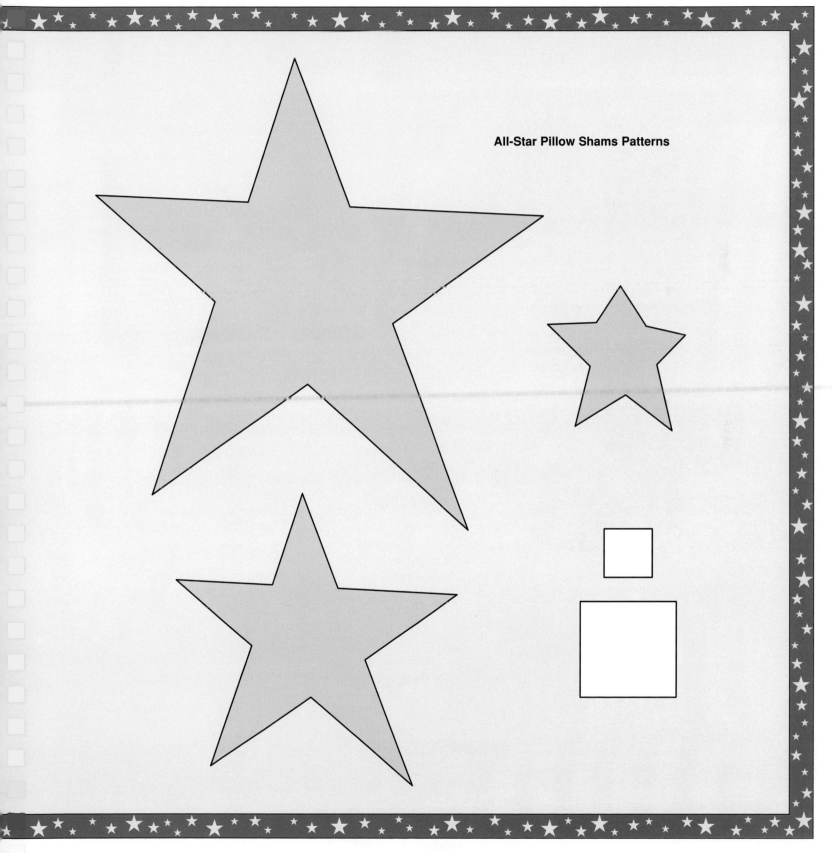

All-Star Pillow Shams Patterns

Floral Ribbon Afghans

Add a touch of glamour to an oh-so-soft chenille afghan by embellishing it with delicate flowers and simple stitches made of ribbon.

WHAT YOU'LL NEED
Purchased ribbon butterflies, flowers, and ladybugs or desired ribbons to make pattern desired; thread
Non-woven interfacing
Purchased evenweave chenille afghan
Two ½- to 1½-inch-wide ribbons twice as wide as the afghan for borders
Medium crochet hook

HERE'S HOW
1. To make a ribbon rose (*opposite and below*), begin with 1 yard of 1½-inch-wide sheer ribbon. Fold the right end down so it extends ½ inch below the selvage. Roll the right end in several turns and secure with stitches. Fold the left end of the ribbon toward the center, roll a few times, and secure. Fold the ribbon end in the opposite direction again, roll (leaving about 12 inches unrolled), and stitch in place. Stitch the bottom edge of the rolled ribbon to the center of the interfacing. Sew a gathering thread along the bottom of the remaining ribbon. Gather ribbon around the center, stitching to the interfacing. Trim excess interfacing. For leaves, fold desired ribbon into a "figure eight" securing in the center. Stitch leaves to the back of the interfacing. Stitch the roses to the afghan where desired.
2. To make a straight woven border, weave the ribbon in and out of the afghan parallel to the afghan edge. Weave the tails into the afghan to secure. Add ribbon roses as for Step 1, omitting the leaves.
3. To work ribbon cross-stitches on the afghan, start four threads up and four threads in from the left fringed edge. Use a crochet hook to pull the ribbon through the afghan from the back to the front. Count eight rows up and eight rows over and pull the ribbon to the backside. Work the ribbon under four threads horizontally and work another half cross-stitch in the opposite direction. Continue to make half cross-stitches until the opposite side is reached. Complete the Xs by crossing the first row of stitches. Use thread to tack on purchased or handmade ribbon embellishments.

OPPOSITE Large roses are made by rolling wide ribbon into the shape of a rose, stitching the rolled end together, and adding a leaf.

BELOW LEFT Variegated ribbon fences in dainty rainbow-colored blooms made in the same manner as the roses.

BELOW RIGHT Gold-edged lavender and white Xs create the background for purchased ribbon bugs and blossoms.

OUR THREE VERSIONS
For the rose scheme
Green, red, and lavender
For the rainbow color scheme
Variegated, blue, yellow, lavender, and pink
For bugs and blossoms scheme
Purple, lavender, yellow, red, white, green, and metallic gold

Quilted Yo-Yo Edgings

Sew up a set of these yo-yo trimmed pillowcases that invite guests to sleep well and come back soon.

OUR THREE VERSIONS
For the pastel color scheme
Light blues, pinks, yellows, lavenders, and white
For the bright color scheme
Reds, blues, teal, and white
For the neutral color scheme
Cream, tan, blue, lavender, yellow, red, and ochre

WHAT YOU'LL NEED
Tracing paper
Pencil
Scissors
⅛ yard each of 6 to 8 different cotton calico fabrics
Needle
Sewing thread to match fabrics
Purchased flat sheet or pillowcase
¾-inch-wide flat braid

OPPOSITE Soft pink solid and checked fabrics make a lovely background for the pastel yo-yos.

ABOVE Natural tones team up with blues, yellows, and lavenders for a garden-and-earth combination.

ABOVE RIGHT Bright yo-yos make a cheerful wake-up call.

Quilted Yo-Yo Edgings

HERE'S HOW

▼ **1.** Trace the desired size circle pattern, *opposite*, onto tracing paper and cut out. Trace around circle onto fabric and cut out.

▼ **2.** Finger press a scant ¼ inch under along the outside edge. With a double thread, work a running stitch along the folded edge.

▲ **3.** Gather tightly and secure the thread. Make several yo-yos.
▶ **4.** Sew the yo-yos together by hand-tacking them at the edges.
5. Align the yo-yos along the hemmed edge of the sheet or pillowcase and hand-tack in place. Sew flat braid next to the last row of yo-yos.

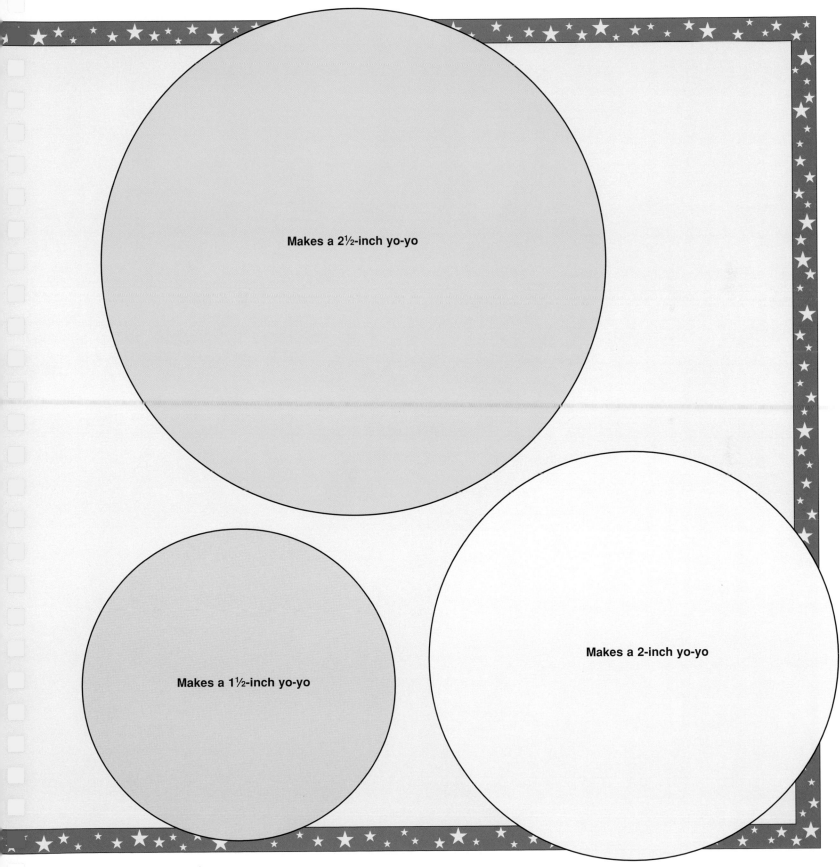

Makes a 2½-inch yo-yo

Makes a 2-inch yo-yo

Makes a 1½-inch yo-yo

Hankie-Trimmed Pillows

Antique buttons, purchased appliquéd letters, and vintage hankies all combine to make clever pillows that will be treasured forever.

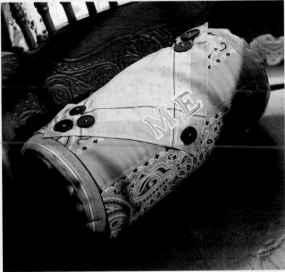

WHAT YOU'LL NEED

For Rectangular Pillow
Purchased rectangular
   pillow in desired color
Square hanky with rose
   motif in center
Crocheted edging
Assorted buttons
Perle cotton
Purchased press-on
   appliqué letter for initial
¼-inch ribbon
For Bolster Pillow
Purchased bolster pillow
   in desired color
Bandanna hankie
Smaller plaid hankie
Purchased press-on appliqué letters
   for initials
Black buttons
Black embroidery floss
For Square Pillow
Purchased square pillow in desired
   color
Two sizes of hankies
Purchased press-on appliqué letters
   for initials
Assorted buttons
Embroidery floss

HERE'S HOW

1. *For the Rectangular Pillow:* Press under a corner of the hankie. Stitch trim to hankie edge. Thread buttons onto ribbon and stitch to the hankie. Accent the flowers on the hankie with French knots made with perle cotton. Fuse the monogram to the front. Stitch hankie fold to the top of the pillow.

2. *For the Bolster Pillow:* Wrap the bandanna around the pillow. Overlap the edges and stitch to secure. Fuse the letters onto a corner of the hankie. Attach the hankie to the pillow using buttons and running stitches.

OUR THREE VERSIONS
For rectangular pillow
Blue, black, red, yellow, white, pink, and green
For bolster pillow
Yellow, blue, white, and black
For square pillow
Green, rust, peach, and white

OPPOSITE A beautiful use of vintage materials, this pillow can be just as sweet using present-day supplies.

LEFT Purchased appliqués add personalization to this pillow accented with a yellow bandanna.

ABOVE This pillow top uses overlapping handkerchiefs and fuses the letters in a diagonal fashion.

3. *For the Square Pillow:* Stitch buttons to the corners of the larger hankie, securing it to the pillow. Following the manufacturer's instructions, fuse the letters to the second hankie top where desired. Sew the top hankie to the pillow using buttons as shown.

come outside with me

Our yards, our gardens, our porches, and our patios are all an extension of the nests we call home. To make your outdoor haven as exciting as each room of the house, we gathered together sunny projects for your outdoor living. These fun ideas will make your moments with nature even more memorable.

Citronella Candleholders

Perched on weather-worn driftwood branches, these whimsical candleholders will help to keep the bugs away while your garden is aglow with light and color.

WHAT YOU'LL NEED

Driftwood branches or stumps; saw
Acrylic paints in desired colors
Plate for palette; paintbrush
6- or 4-inch clay pot saucers
Clay pot, if desired
Flat, round, and outlining brushes
Liquid Nails® adhesive

OPPOSITE A gnarly stump holds this terra-cotta saucer painted like summer's watermelon.

BELOW The pastel pot matches the saucer with a pretty pink citronella candle inside.

RIGHT This bright pair sits naturally on a Y-shaped driftwood branch.

HERE'S HOW

1. Choose a piece of driftwood large enough to hold a clay saucer. Use a saw to cut off the top of the driftwood as level as possible. When choosing a length of driftwood to insert into the ground, allow for about 14 inches to be buried under the ground.
2. Place a small amount of each color of paint onto a plate for painting. Paint the base and lip of the clay saucer using solid colors as desired and let the paint dry. Paint stripes, dots, and lines over the solid areas. Allow the paint to dry.
3. Holding the driftwood upright, position the saucer onto the top of the wood. Apply a generous amount of adhesive to the wood surface where the clay saucer will be placed. *(Note: You will have plenty of time to work with this adhesive before it sets, but once it sets, it is permanent.)*
4. If desired, dig a hole in the ground about 14 inches deep. Insert the citronella holder. Pack dirt in firmly around the driftwood. Place a candle and holder or candle only onto the saucer or into the pot.

OUR THREE VERSIONS
Bright color scheme
Red, blue, black, white, and lime green
Pastel color scheme
Soft yellow, pink, and soft lime green
Natural color scheme
Dark green, brick red, ochre, and black

Cheery Cherry Birdhouses

These irresistible birdhouses add charm to the garden and welcome small birds in grand style.

WHAT YOU'LL NEED

12x12-inch piece of ¼-inch
  plywood
Tracing paper
Carbon paper
Jigsaw
Drill and drill bits
Wood glue
1-inch brad nails
Hammer
Acrylic paints in desired colors,
  plus red and green
1-inch flat and small round
  paintbrushes
Crackling medium
Round pencil-tip eraser
Black permanent fine-tip marker
Sandpaper

OPPOSITE The red roof and checkered border bring out the color of the miniature cherries.

ABOVE To achieve a vivid crackling effect, choose colors high in contrast, like white and deep turquoise.

ABOVE RIGHT Crackles of gold and white give this birdhouse a country flair.

OUR THREE VERSIONS

For the primary color scheme
Red, white, black, and green
For the bright color scheme
Turquoise, white, red, black,
and green
For the country color scheme
Gold, white, red, black, and green

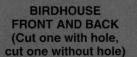

**BIRDHOUSE
FRONT AND BACK
(Cut one with hole,
cut one without hole)**

**BIRDHOUSE SIDE
(Cut two)**

Cheery Cherry
Birdhouses

HERE'S HOW

1. Trace the patterns, *pages 66–67*, onto tracing paper. Transfer the outlines to the plywood using carbon paper. Using a jigsaw, cut the pieces according to the pattern.

2. Drill a ⅞-inch-diameter hole in the front piece as shown on the pattern.

3. Attach the side edge of each side piece to the front using glue and two brad nails. Attach the back to edges of side pieces in the same manner. Glue the smaller roof piece in place, taking care to align top edge with point on front and back. Secure it with brads. Glue and nail the remaining roof piece, with the top edge overlapping first roof piece. Apply bead of glue along bottom edges of assembly all around, attach bottom and secure with brads.

4. Paint the base coats in the desired colors. If using the crackling technique, the base coats will show up as cracks during the process. Let the paint dry. Paint checked patterns on the birdhouse edges, if desired.

5. Paint all surfaces with crackling medium where the crackling effect is desired. Let the crackling medium dry.

▲ **6.** Using a flat brush, apply the contrasting top coat of paint using long straight strokes. Do not repaint any wet areas or the crackling process will not work. Paint the areas desired and allow the paint to dry.

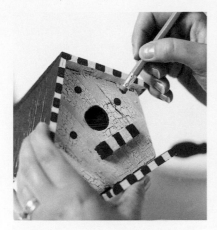

▲ 7. To make cherries, dip the eraser end of a pencil into red paint. Dab it on the birdhouse where cherry motifs are desired. Using a round-tip brush, add green leaves.

▼ 8. Using a black permanent marker, draw in stems about ½-inch long. Sand the edges of the birdhouse to achieve a weathered look.

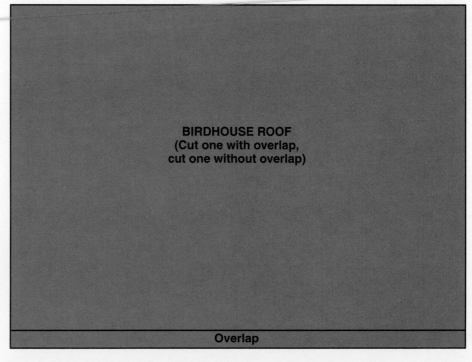

BIRDHOUSE BASE
(Cut one)

BIRDHOUSE ROOF
(Cut one with overlap,
cut one without overlap)

Overlap

Flower Pot Fountains

Your family and friends will bubble over with delight when they see this playful fountain made from used-to-be-ordinary terra-cotta pots.

WHAT YOU'LL NEED
Acrylic paints; paintbrush
16-inch terra-cotta saucer base
10-inch terra-cotta azalea pot
6-inch terra-cotta azalea pot
4-inch terra-cotta pot
1½-inch terra-cotta pot
Small cement or waterproof pot feet
Round pencil-tip eraser, paintbrush, or wooden dowel
Submersible pump with bell fountain head
Purchased wooden shape for top
Dowel
Modeling clay; clear silicone sealer
1-inch-thick Styrofoam
Liquid Nails clear weatherproof adhesive
Marbles

OPPOSITE Black and white marbles fill this delightful fountain for a whimsical garden accessory.

RIGHT Topped with a polka-dot star, each stacked pot has vivid triangle motifs bordering the brim.

FAR RIGHT Painted flowers atop pastel stripes give the impression of a white picket fence in the garden.

Important notes: Select the terra-cotta pots and saucers carefully. Pots often have cracks in them, but be sure that the base and large pot are free of cracks. These pots will have various size holes. Purchase the pump and fountain first. Take the stem from the fountain and make sure it fits through the holes in the bottoms of the three large pots. Place pump in water, add fountain and turn it on before beginning this project so that you are familiar with how it works and know how to adjust it. Also read all of the instructions for safety and maintenance.

OUR THREE VERSIONS
Bright polka-dot scheme
Red, yellow, grass green, purple, hot pink, black, white, and orange
Stars scheme
Ochre gold, purple, olive green, rust red, and black,
Pastel floral scheme
Peachy pink,
lavender, yellow,
soft moss green,
soft baby blue,
and white

Flower Pot Fountains

HERE'S HOW:

1. Paint the pots, saucer, dowels, wood toppers, and figurines the desired colors. Paint about 2 inches of the inside rim of pot. Paint desired motifs on the pots. To add dots, dip the end of a dowel, paintbrush, or pencil eraser into paint and dab on the surface. Let it dry.

▲ **2.** Insert the pump. Place the pump inside the large pot, inserting the cord through the hole in the bottom. Use a non-hardening oil-based modeling clay to seal the hole around the cord and form a base to hold the pump in place. Position the pump so that the stem will come up in the center.

▶ **3.** Carefully turn the pot over, resting it on something to hold the pump in place. Seal the bottom thoroughly with clear silicone sealer. Allow it to set for 24 hours.

▲ **4.** Position the large pot in the saucer. Use the painted characters (pot feet) or small rocks to accommodate the cord and level the pot.

5. Cut the Styrofoam rings to act as risers inside the pots. (Use Styrofoam purchased in a crafts store or 1-inch-thick insulation Styrofoam purchased at a home improvement center which is less expensive for a larger amount.) Cut the first circle to fit about 2 inches below the top of pot. Cut another circle or two to raise the second pot to the desired height. Cut center holes to allow the stem to go through the Styrofoam. Clean off any Styrofoam crumbs before inserting in the pot. Keep the water free of debris that could clog the pump.

▲ **6.** Stack the second pot atop the first.

▼ **7.** Repeat the process for the next level. Add the third pot and place the fountain head onto the stem.

▲ 8. A fourth pot and a painted topper glued to a dowel may be glued to the top of fountain head, if desired. Allow the adhesive to set.

▼ 9. Test the fountain and make pressure adjustments on the pump and fountain head If needed. Fill the 10-inch pot with water up to the point of the Styrofoam. It is important to fill it deep enough to keep the pump well submerged at all times and allow time for the water to rise up and flow down into the base pot. Adjust the head so the water flows just over the top pot, into the second pot and flows smoothly down the sides. *Do not* allow a lot of splattering outside the base pot; it is important to keep water contained in the large pot.

▲ 10. When the fountain flows as desired, add marbles to cover all of the Styrofoam.

RIGHT Fountain pumps come in a variety of styles; shown is a submersible pump with a bell fountain head.

BELOW RIGHT "Pot feet" come in all shapes and can be painted. They are available at garden centers.

Porch Chair Friends

Mary Engelbreit has designed these springtime friends just for you—to perch upon your chair and keep you company.

WHAT YOU'LL NEED
³⁄₁₆-inch-thick wood
Tracing paper; scissors; pencil
Sandpaper; wood glue
Decorative plastic coated wire
Wooden beads
½-inch wooden plug
For the bee: Acrylic paints in yellow, black, white, and blue
For the bird: Acrylic paints in black, orange, blue, pink, and white
For the butterfly: Acrylic paints in yellow, orange, red, blue, and lime green

HERE'S HOW
1. Purchase enough ³⁄₁₆-inch-thick wood to cut as many shapes as you wish. Use the patterns, *pages 74–75*, as a guide.
2. Transfer the desired patterns onto tracing paper and cut out. Trace onto wood and cut out. Sand the edges.
3. *To paint the bee:* Paint the body yellow and the tail, two beads, and stripes black. To paint the wings, first paint the entire wing white. To add shading, blend paint on the wood while paint is still wet. Use a very small touch of blue on tip of brush and brush into the wet white, brushing from the top of wings downward fading into white. Glue black stripes on, add wires and beads, reinforcing with a small dab of glue.

4. *To paint the bird:* Use the same shading technique. Paint the breast area pink adding white shading toward the blue area. Add white shading to the blue areas lightening the ends of the feathers on wings and tail. Paint black eyes and orange beak. Using wood glue, attach wings.
5. *To paint the butterfly:* Paint the entire piece yellow, add orange shading. Paint on dots and colored areas. Paint body, head and beads green. Let dry and attach with glue.
6. Drill tiny holes in wood, attaching wires and reinforcing them with glue.

OPPOSITE This buzzing fellow has dimensional black stripes and beads held by spiralled wires.

OUR THREE VERSIONS
For the bee
Yellow, black, white, and light blue
For the bird
Orange, blue, pink, and white
For the butterfly
Yellow, orange, red, blue, and green

ABOVE LEFT With wings ready to glide on the breeze, this bird appears to be landing on the chair's back.

ABOVE You'll want to study this vividly detailed butterfly that looks like it is in motion.

Porch Chair Friend Buzzing Bee

Porch Chair Friend Blue Bird

WING
Cut 2

Porch Chair Friend Happy Butterfly

Blooming Garden Posts

Treat your garden to this painted sign that has a create-it-yourself weathered look.

WHAT YOU'LL NEED

Green treated decorative deck post
Acrylic paints
Paintbrush
Foam bowl
Water
Sandpaper
Clear varnish
Green treated board approximately
   5¼x20 inches
Tracing paper
Pencil
Two hook screws
2 yards
  of twine

OUR THREE VERSIONS

For the white pole
White, purple, red, ochre, green,
and black
For the red pole
Red, black, ochre, white, and green
For the lavender pole
Lavender, bright pink, black, blue,
white, and green

OPPOSITE The weathered white post
looks at home in this lavish garden.

LEFT Pretty enough for a child's
butterfly garden, this color combination
is as fresh as spring itself.

FAR LEFT Muted country
colors adorn this rustic
post and sign.

Blooming Garden Posts

HERE'S HOW

▼ **1.** Mix paint in a bowl, thinning it to about two parts water and one part paint. Paint the post using vertical strokes until covered. The paint should cover but still be transparent enough to see wood grain. If the color appears too transparent, give it another coat. Let the paint dry. Add the accent colors of trim to ridged areas over the base color. Let the paint dry thoroughly.

2. Use a medium-grit sandpaper to lightly sand the entire post, especially the raised areas, corners of post, and edges, until the bare wood shows through. Brush off all dust and coat with clear varnish.

3. For the sign board, paint the base color first. Paint the outline, rectangle, corner square, and checks along the edges. (These don't have to be perfectly shaped, straight, or smooth lines.)

▼ **4.** Trace the patterns (matching A/B to A/B and C/D to C/D), *right and opposite*, onto tracing paper. Transfer the design onto the painted board by

coloring the back of the tracing paper with a soft pencil. Position the pattern onto the board and outline with a sharp pencil. Paint the letters and the flower.

5. Finish the sign the same way as the post. Sand the entire surface and edges. Brush off the dust. Apply varnish to the sign and let it dry.

6. Screw in hook screws and pull twine through. Tie it to desired length, and trim off excess. Hang the sign on the post.

treat your windows

Frame your windows to the world with curtains and trims that will bring you joy on even the cloudiest of days. You'll be delighted with fresh new ideas for shutters, tiebacks, valances, and more! Come along as we share "breit" solutions for where the sun shines in.

Whimsy Shutters

Purchased shutters become a blank canvas for adding painted wood pieces in all shapes and sizes.

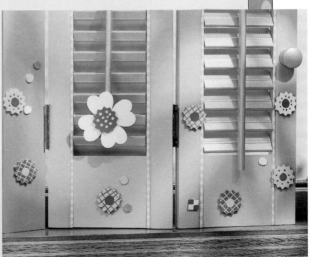

WHAT YOU'LL NEED
Pair of shutters to fit window
Screwdriver
Wooden knobs for handles, optional
Spray paint in desired color
Spray clear acrylic varnish
Acrylic paints in desired colors; paintbrushes
Purchased wood shapes
Thick white crafts glue

HERE'S HOW
1. If painting the shutters, remove the hinges and paint each piece separately. If you are staining, you can stain over the hardware. *(Note: If you do not like the knobs that come with the shutters, purchased wooden knobs can be painted and used.)* The movable slats can be painted easily with spray paint. Just lightly spray, let paint dry, move the slats, spray again, and continue this process until the shutter is evenly covered. The slats also can be painted with acrylic paints and a brush, if desired.

2. After the slats are painted, paint the rest of the shutter as desired using acrylic paints. Use a smaller flat brush to paint the fine ridges and checks. Let the paint dry. Spray with clear varnish and let dry. Reassemble the shutter.

3. Paint the small wood shapes using different colors. Add dots to the shapes by dipping the end of the paintbrush in paint and dotting on the surface. Paint stripes, lines, or whatever you wish. Once dry, spray with varnish and let it dry.

4. Glue the shapes to the shutter as desired. When placing shapes close to the center slats, make sure the shapes do not interfere with opening and closing the slats.

OUR THREE VERSIONS
For the bright color scheme
Bright blue, deep green, magenta, deep purple, yellow, orange, white, black, and lime green
For the country color scheme
Golden oak stain, black, plum, forest green, rust orange, and yellow ochre
For the pastel color scheme
Soft blue, soft lime green, lavender, cream, soft yellow, and coral

OPPOSITE In a child's room, these awesome shutters are sure to spark wondrous thoughts.

ABOVE LEFT Sprinkled with falling leaves and squares, polka-dot pulls complete the look.

ABOVE These playful shutters allow in plenty of sunshine while keeping out glaring rays.

Simple Napkin Curtains

Pieced together, cloth napkins quickly become curtains and look sweet hanging from decorative shower curtain hooks.

WHAT YOU'LL NEED

Fabric napkins, enough to piece
  together to fit the window length
  and desired width
Thread to match napkin fabric
Contrasting rickrack
Grommets and grommet tool
Decorative shower hooks

HERE'S HOW

1. Decide how many napkins are needed for each curtain. Overlap the hems, and stitch the horizontal napkins together in a patchwork style. Stitch the vertical seams.

2. Add grommets 1 inch from the top edge of the curtain, spaced about 6 inches apart. Attach the curtains to the rod using decorative shower hooks.

OUR THREE VERSIONS

For the seaside scheme
Bright blue, white, and yellow
For the flower pot scheme
Red, chambray, yellow, white, and gold
For the roses scheme
Navy blue and white

OPPOSITE Held in place by a school of fish, these plaid curtains are oh-so-clever with a simple handwritten verse framing the window.

ABOVE Soft stripes are topped with miniature bouquets to create a window treatment that will add a touch of spring to any room.

ABOVE RIGHT Navy and white pair up beautifully to make striking curtains that are blooming with roses.

Bottle-It-Up Tie Backs

Wrapped in wire to hold curtains in place, lightweight bottles and vases are filled with fresh flowers for all to enjoy.

WHAT YOU'LL NEED

Small, lightweight bottle or vase
Contact paper and/or vinyl
  reinforcements
Scissors; etching cream
Armature wire; thin plastic-wrapped
  colored wire, if desired
Needle-nose pliers
Large staples or cup hooks

HERE'S HOW

1. Wash the bottle or vase thoroughly and allow it to dry.
2. Cut small shapes from the Contact paper and apply to the bottle as desired. To make a checkerboard, use small squares. To make dots, use reinforcements. The uncovered areas will become the etched areas.
3. Etch the glass following the manufacturer's instructions. Allow the etching cream to work and rinse as recommended. Remove all Contact paper.

4. Cut a piece of armature wire approximately 24 inches long. If desired, wrap one end with colored wire.
5. Make a coil about the size of a nickel at one end of the wire. Begin to wrap the bottle or vase, placing the coil at the bottom for support, if necessary.
6. Bend the remaining wire in a zigzag manner. Using pliers, make a small loop approximately 5 inches from the end. Make a coil at the end.
7. Attach to the wall or woodwork by affixing the back wire flat to the surface with large staples or two large cup hooks.

OUR THREE VERSIONS

For the colored bottle tie back
Royal blue and silver
For the clear vase tie back
Silver and orange
For the green-tinted bottle tie back
Silver and teal

OPPOSITE An etched checkerboard neck is the perfect finishing touch to this brilliant blue bottle.

ABOVE The armature wire is wrapped in green crafting wire to accentuate the green tint in the glass.

ABOVE LEFT This once ordinary vase is transformed into a tie back with a handful of supplies and a few simple steps.

Have-a-Notion Trims

Head to the notion box to make these delightful curtains with tabs loaded with personality plus.

WHAT YOU'LL NEED

Fabric for curtain (window height plus 1 inch for length; 1½ times window width for curtain width)

Contrasting fabric for tabs and backing

Decorative buttons or blanket pins with charms

HERE'S HOW

For the button tabs

1. To hem the curtain sides, fold ¼ inch of each edge to the back. Repeat and stitch in place. Hem the bottom edge of the curtain in the same manner.

2. Enlarge pattern, *right*, onto tracing paper and cut out. Place the pattern over the facing fabric and trace the tabbed part of the header, repeating across the width of the facing. Cut out. Repeat for the top of the curtain fabric. Cut out.

3. With right sides facing, stitch the facing to the curtain using a ¼-inch seam allowance. Trim and clip the seams. Turn right side out and press.

4. Fold the tabs over to the front and secure in place by sewing a button or pin to the center through all layers.

OUR THREE VERSIONS

For the sheer star scheme
Ivory and metallic gold
For the round stacked button scheme
Yellow, green, and red
For the yo-yo and pansy scheme
Black, lavender, yellow, and red

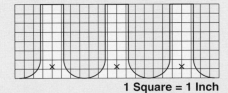

1 Square = 1 Inch

OPPOSITE Create a heavenly look for any room with starry fabric and secure the tabs with celestial themed pins.

ABOVE LEFT Accented with green tabs and yellow and red buttons, this calico curtain would look quaint hanging from a painted rod.

ABOVE These fun curtains go up in a jiffy with tabs that secure with purchased yo-yos and pansy buttons.

Shelf Toppers

While curtains blow in the breeze below, these fun curtain toppers hold treasured collections up high.

WHAT YOU'LL NEED

Purchased wood shelf
  with Shaker pegs
Acrylic paint in desired
  color
Acrylic spray varnish
Sandpaper
Fabric for curtain (window
  height plus 8 inches for
  length; shelf width plus
  1 inch, plus 3 inches for
  each pleat/Shaker peg
  for width)
Fabric for bow

HERE'S HOW

1. To hem the curtain sides, fold ¼ inch of each edge to the back. Repeat and stitch in place. Hem the bottom edge of the curtain in the same manner.

2. Zigzag stitch the top edge of the curtain. Press 4 inches at the top to the back.

3. Evenly space box pleats by each Shaker peg across the curtain top. Machine-stitch pleats 1 inch down from the top edge.

4. To make hanging loops from contrasting fabric, cut a 1x6-inch strip for each loop. Fold a strip in half and stitch along long edge using a ¼-inch seam allowance. Turn right side out. Fold the loop in half and stitch the ends to the back side of the pleat, adjusting to the desired length. Repeat for each hanging loop.

5. To make bows from contrasting fabric, cut a 1½x30-inch strip for each bow. Fold a strip in half and stitch along long edge using a ¼-inch seam allowance. Turn right side out. Knot the ends of the strip. Tie the strip into a bow and stitch to the center of the pleat. Repeat for each bow.

OUR THREE VERSIONS

For the teacup scheme
Red and black
For the kitchen accessory scheme
Pale yellow, white, and green
For the '50s scheme
Bright pink and black

OPPOSITE Soft and sweet, the greens and yellows in these curtains and shelf are right at home in any room of the house.

ABOVE LEFT It's always tea time with this fun window covering that also displays lovely china.

ABOVE Girls of all ages will squeal with delight at this window treatment that rocks and rolls with '50s appeal.

little
extras

I t's those little accents—an unexpected trim on the front door or a

grouping of photographs framed in an eye-catching way—that make a

home a personal reflection of you. The fun begins on the next page

with a wonderful collection of special "ah-has" for your walls,

tabletops, and doors.

Personality Purses

*Express your creativity by welcoming visitors to your house
with these door decorations that are such fun to make.*

WHAT YOU'LL NEED
Old purse
Styrofoam
Thin wire, if desired
Mary Engelbreit greeting card
Tape
Wooden crafts sticks
Embellishments such as
   artificial flowers, fabric
   swatches, feathers,
   necklaces, and scarves
Scissors

HERE'S HOW
1. Insert a block of Styrofoam
into the purse. Fit it inside to
fill the space snugly but not
to make it bulge.
2. The purse handle itself can be
used as a hanger. For extra support,
make a loop from thin wire and attach
it to the top center of the purse back.
3. Insert desired items into the purse,
beginning with the card. Tape a crafts
stick to the card back and stick it into
the Styrofoam as desired. Next add
items around the card, using fabric,
feathers, flowers, jewelry, fake fur, or
whatever you wish. Attach wires on
each side of a necklace and drape
from side to side. Swatches of fabric
can be inserted by folding corners
together, tying with a wire and
inserting into the Styrofoam.

OPPOSITE A golden evening bag holds
feathers and frills to "tickle" guests.

ABOVE The rich colors of this
arrangement accent one of Mary
Engelbreit's greeting cards.

ABOVE RIGHT Bold polka-dot fabric
adds contrast to the natural woven
straw purse.

Scarves or fur trim also can be stuffed
and draped behind the card. Feathers
may be glued on the back of the card
or any smooth surface. Insert tall
flowers behind the card.

OUR THREE VERSIONS
For gold purse
Mauve, blue, and turquoise
feathers
Pink, blue, and white pearls
Gold beads
White fur
White lace
Peach and ivory satin
White silk flowers
For red purse
Purple, gold, black, and turquoise
necklaces
Purple and red flowers
Multicolored jewel-tone scarves
Forest green satin
Royal blue feathers
For straw purse
Red and white polka-dot fabric
Yellow calico fabric
Black with multi bright colored
dotted fabric
Red, yellow green, white, and
black beads
Yellow and white flowers
Blue and red feathers

Sweet Cherry Jars

Painted cherries and dots add a cheerful touch to a glass candy jar.

WHAT YOU'LL NEED
Newspapers
Purchased glass candy jar
   with lid
Paintbrushes
Liquitex Glossies glass paint

OPPOSITE This squatty jar
has a lid with a round knob,
perfect for painting a cherry
on the top.

RIGHT Highly contrasting
colors of yellow and black
make the dots and cherries
show up vividly on this jar.

FAR RIGHT Metallic gold
dots frame these cherries
painted with rich tones of
red and green.

OUR THREE VERSIONS
For Southwestern color scheme
Aqua, blue green, black, white,
and red purple
For bright color scheme
Yellow, red, black, green, and white
For neutral color scheme
Golden brown, almond, pine
green, maroon, black, metallic gold,
and white

Sweet Cherry Jars

HERE'S HOW

1. Cover the work surface with newspaper. Paint the jar base and lid using contrasting colors of glass paint. Let the paint dry thoroughly.

◄ **2.** Using a shade of red, paint random cherry shapes, about the size of a nickel, on the jar base. If the lid has a round knob, paint the knob red. Let the paint dry. If necessary, paint a second coat on the cherries and let the paint dry.

3. Paint one or two desired leaf shapes above each cherry and randomly place a few. Let the paint dry.

▲ **4.** Paint stems to connect the leaves to the cherries. Let the paint dry.

◀ **5.** Use black paint and a fine liner paintbrush to outline the cherries, leaves, and veins.

▼ **6.** To paint polkadots, dip the handle end of the paintbrush into the paint. Dab onto jar and lid surfaces. Let the paint dry.

▲ **7.** Use white paint to add highlights to the cherries as desired.

Memory Frames

A few snips here, a little glue there, and you'll have a picture mat that beams with personality.

WHAT YOU'LL NEED

Small pointed scissors
Mary Engelbreit wrapping paper
Purchased frame with picture
 mat to fit
Paper doilies in desired shapes
 and colors
Decoupage medium
Flat paintbrush
Acrylic paint in desired color

HERE'S HOW

1. Cut out desired motifs from wrapping paper, trimming edges carefully and as close to the outline of the image as possible.
2. Determine placement of each cutout piece and of the doilies. The pieces can overlap. If necessary, trim the doilies to fit the picture mat. Glue the pieces in place using decoupage medium. Paint the entire front of the picture mat with a coat of decoupage medium and let it dry. Give the mat a second coat and let it dry.
3. To add small dots between paper designs, dip the handle end of the paintbrush into acrylic paint and dot it on the surface of the mat where dots are desired. Let the paint dry.

OPPOSITE This frame encloses a double picture mat that helps separate the photos from the decorated mat.

ABOVE Mary's colorful wrapping paper designs pop off the whimsical black and white background.

ABOVE RIGHT The olive mat, gold doilies, and wood frame bring out the natural tones of the paper cutouts.

OUR THREE VERSIONS

For the pastel color scheme
Lime green, cream, and light blue
For the contemporary color scheme
Black and white
For the natural tone color scheme
Metallic gold, deep green, and golden brown

Beribboned Tassels

Hanging from a door knob, these dancing tassels are topped with a wooden finial that holds loops of ribbon and other little surprises.

WHAT YOU'LL NEED

Wooden finial
Wire cutter and sandpaper,
  if necessary
Small screw eye
Acrylic paint; paintbrush
Scissors
1½ yards each of three wired
  ribbons in different patterns,
  colors, and widths
White fabric crafts glue
Beads and cording for hanging
Embellishments as desired
Clear gloss spray

OUR THREE VERSIONS

For the pastel color scheme
Pink, cream, and mauve
For the two-tone color scheme
Mauve and metallic gold
For the bright color scheme
Purple, fuchsia, lime green, white,
and yellow

OPPOSITE Small dainty pearls top
this soft colored tassel.

RIGHT Golden stars fall from striped
and polka-dot ribbons.

ABOVE RIGHT A multi-colored and
whimsically painted finial is the
finishing touch to this merry tassel.

Beribboned Tassels

HERE'S HOW

1. If the finial has a screw in the bottom end, cut it off with a wire cutter. Lightly sand the wood. Screw the screw eye to the center top of the finial.

2. Paint the finial in desired color of acrylic paint. Allow the paint to dry and spray only the top half with clear gloss.

3. Cut the ribbons for the first two layers into six 9-inch lengths. Cut the top layer, the narrowest ribbon, into 8-inch lengths.

▲ **4.** Bring the ends of the ribbon together to form a loop and glue the ends together. For the wider ribbons (1 inch and wider) take a little pleat in each end before gluing the ends together. Let the loops dry.

▲ **5.** Evenly space and glue the six loops of one ribbon around the neck of the finial. Allow the glue to dry. Glue six loops of the second ribbon on top of the first loops, offsetting them slightly. When dry, glue the final, narrowest ribbon around the neck.

▶ **6.** Glue a narrow strip of ribbon around the neck to cover the raw edges of the ribbon loops.

▲ **7.** To embellish the tassel, slip beads onto the narrow ribbon, glue loops of beads on a string on top of the ribbon loops, glue sequins to the finial, or string objects on a cord and use a thumbtack to attach them to the bottom of the finial, under the ribbons.

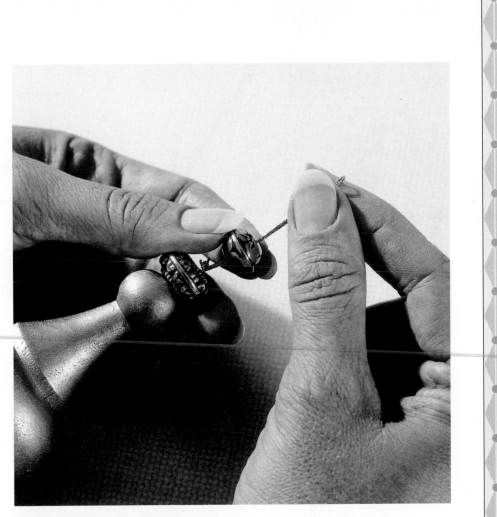

▲ **8.** Thread a length of cord through the screw eye. Slip decorative beads onto the cord and knot the cord to prevent beads from falling off. *(Note: If the first bead has a large enough hole, it will slip over the screw eye to hide it.)* Tie the ends of the cord together to make a hanging loop.

Pretty Painted Vases

Tiny vases make a big impact when striking flowers are painted front and center.

WHAT YOU'LL NEED
Glass vase
Water and dish soap
Pencil and tracing paper
Scissors; tape
Paintbrush
Liquitex® Glossies™ glass paints in
   desired colors
Ribbon, optional

HERE'S HOW
1. Wash the vase and let it dry. Be careful not to touch the area that is going to be painted.
2. Trace the desired pattern, *right*, onto tracing paper and cut out the shape around the outside outline *only*.
3. Use small rings of tape on the back of the pattern to position it on the front of the bottle. Use a fine paintbrush and black paint to paint around the pattern. Carefully remove the pattern. Let the paint dry.
4. Paint in the flower and leaves using the desired colors. Let the paint dry. Use a fine paintbrush to add in the black line details. Let the paint dry.
5. Bake the glass piece in the oven to heat-set the paint if recommended by the paint manufacturer. Let the piece cool. Tie a bow around the neck of the vase, if desired.

OUR THREE VERSIONS
For the pink
rose scheme
Pink, yellow-orange,
green, and black
For the orange
posy scheme
Orange, yellow, black,
and green
For the white daisy scheme
White, yellow, green, and black

OPPOSITE Triangular colored vases (found in a discount or crafts store) are just big enough to present colorful blooms.

FAR LEFT Fresh from the garden, these daisies are delightful in a matching vase.

LEFT One of Mary Engelbreit's favorites, this cottage rose is pretty painted in any color combination.

Credits

PHOTOGRAPHERS:
Andy Lyons Cameraworks: pages
14–15, 18–19, 22–23, 25, 32–33,
36–37, 38, 40, 46–47, 50, 54–55, 56,
58–59, 64–65, 66–67, 70–71, 72–73,
80, 84, 88–89, 90–91, 92–93, 98–99
100–101, 108–109

Bill Hopkins Associates: pages 86–87

Scott Little: pages 10–11, 12, 16–17,
20–21, 23, 24, 30–31, 44–45, 48–49,
52–53, 62–63, 68–69, 71, 78–79, 85,
96–97, 102–103, 104–105, 106–107

PHOTOSTYLING ASSISTANT:
Donna Chesnut

DESIGNERS:
Susan Banker: pages 10, 14, 30, 32,
64, 88, 98, 102, 108

Carol Dahlstrom: page 40

Phyllis Dunstan: pages 36, 104

Margaret Sindelar: pages 24, 52, 54,
58, 86, 90, 92

Alice Wetzel: pages 16, 20, 40, 44,
48, 62, 68, 78, 84, 96

Index